Copyright © 2021 Ericka Mapson.

All rights reserved. This book or any pictures thereof may not be reproduced or used in any manner whatsoever without the express written permission of the publisher except for the use of brief quotations in a book review.

ISBN: 9798688719093

Contributing publisher:

Special Note!

My prayer is that this book will plant the seed that will encourage young boys and girls to travel and explore this great world. I want young people to explore outside of their neighborhoods, burros, towns, cities, states, and/or countries. I want to encourage young people to learn new languages, experience new foods, various cultures, and ways of living their lives.

Don't limit yourself to one state or country. Get out and TRAVEL! Let your imagination run wild. Dream BIG!

Happy traveling little people!

Chapter 1

Mrs. Winter seemed to always find a way to surprise her daughters, Kenya and India. Running Saturday errands could easily turn into a full day adventure, and that morning was no different.

"Hey Mom, where are we going?" Kenya asked.
"Well honey, there is a new donut place called Global Café in downtown Columbus that you guys are going to love!"
"Oooo, I love donuts and books!" India said with excitement.

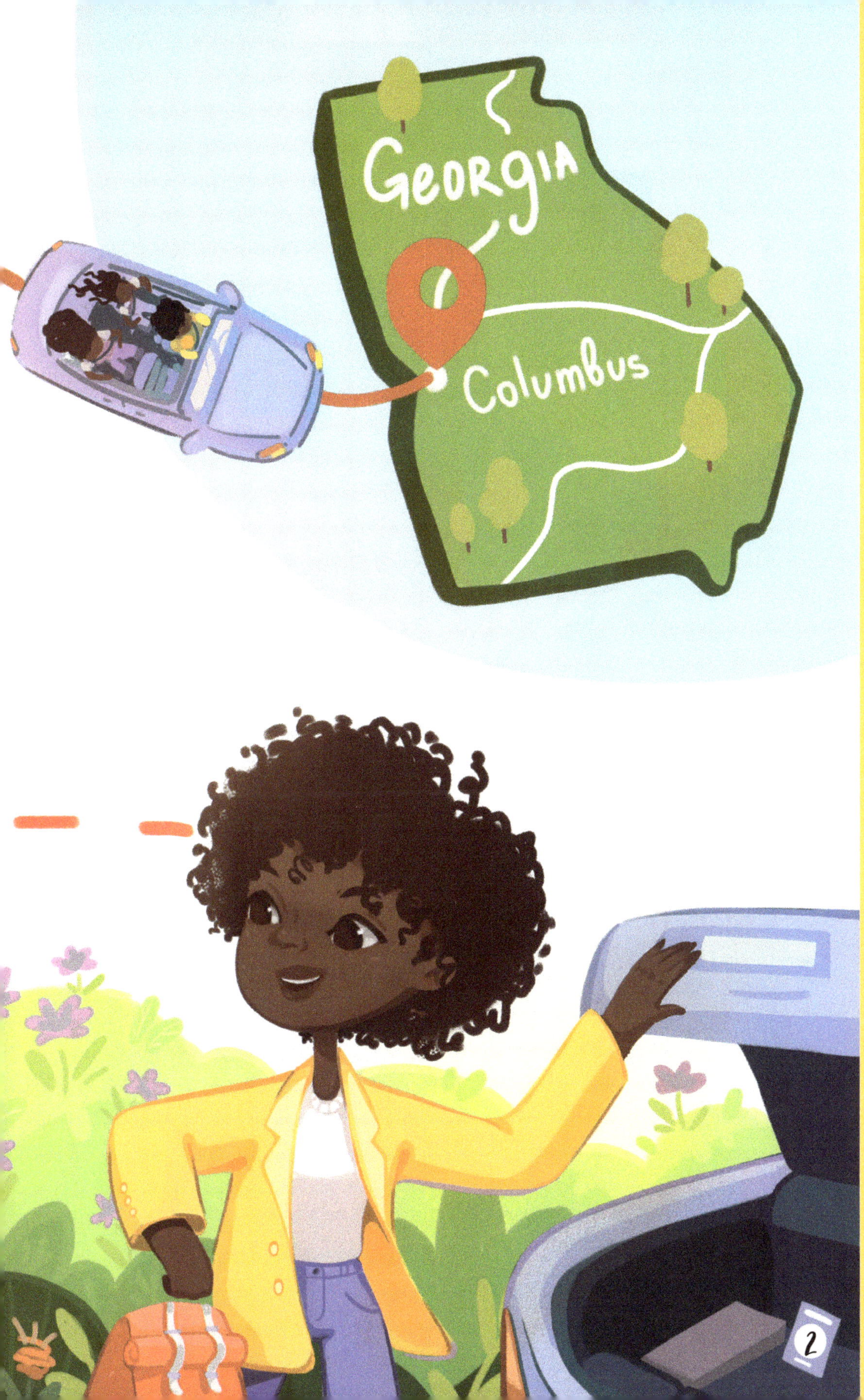
Georgia
Columbus

The girls continued to talk excitedly for the rest of the ride, and before they knew it, their mom was parking the car. They jumped out and started running to the front door.

"Girls, slow down!"
"Okay Mom!"

They walked into the cafe and were shocked. The air smelled like warm, sweet treats. One wall was filled to the ceiling with books and another filled with donuts!

"Mom, this place is amazing!" India exclaimed.
"It has so many books and delicious looking donuts."
"Why are there so many donuts? Not that I'm complaining about it." Kenya chuckled.
"See girls, what makes Global Café so special is its variety of donuts! It has a donut for all 50 states, including the Virgin Islands and its territories!"

The three of them got in line.
"Girls, you can have one donut each. Choose wisely because there's a large selection."
The girls thought carefully before making a decision. There were so many to choose from, making it hard to choose just one.
"Girls, what kind of donut would you like for your snack?"
"May I have the apple donut, please?" Kenya asked.
"And I want an orange donut, please." India chimed in.
"Okay, so a Florida and New York donut," Mom replied.
"No Mom, we said an apple and an orange donut," said Kenya.
"I know honey. New York's nickname is 'The Big Apple', -so it is an apple and cinnamon flavor. Florida is known as the Sunshine state, but is also known for growing citrus fruits, such as oranges, so the Florida donut will taste like an orange with orange slices on the top."
The girls glanced at each other in amazement. How cool is it to order a donut named after a state?

Chapter 2

With their donut choices made, the girls asked their mom if they could go check out books in the children's section. They were so excited to see what new books they could find. Their mom told them to be very quiet because people were working.

Finally, Kenya and India reached the bookshelves and started picking their favorite books. They noticed a girl in a blue outfit reading aloud by the bookshelf. Neither girl recognized her accent and were curious to find out where she was from.

The girls walked over to introduce themselves.
"Hello, my name is Kenya, and this is my sister, India."
"Hi, I'm Carmen!"
"Hi Carmen. Where are you from? Kenya asked.
"I heard you speaking to your mother and noticed you have an accent."
"I do? I never notice when I'm back home." Carmen chuckled.
"I am from London England. It's on the continent of Europe. It's right here." As Carmen pointed to the map on the table, Kenya and India moved in closer to take a look.

"London? You mean where the Queen lives? Do you know her?" India asked in amazement.

"India, don't be silly." Carmen chuckled.

"No, I don't know her personally, but I ride near Buckingham Palace often."

"Wow! You get to see a real palace like every day!" India stated with joy in her voice.

"So, what brings you all the way to Columbus, Georgia?" Kenya inquired.

"My grandparents live here. My parents and I came to visit them while I'm on summer holiday."
"Summer holiday?" India asked.
"We just call it summer vacation."
"So, what do you do for fun here?" Carmen asked.
"Well, we go to summer camp during the day, but we also like to read, play chess, ride our four-wheelers, play outside, and ballet." Kenya said.
"We love to dance."
"What is there to do for fun in London?" asked India.
"We have the same things. We have camp, and I ride my bike and read. I don't do ballet, but I take gymnastics."

"Oh cool," the girls said in unison.
The girls talked about their love of history and museums.

India and Kenya talked about their favorite historical moments like the election of the first Black president, Barack Obama and First Lady Michelle Obama.

They just knew they could do anything they dreamed of in life after that.

Carmen told them all about a giant clock tower called Big Ben, and a huge Ferris wheel called the London Eye.

The girls learned that Carmen loved visiting Georgia, but was really excited to see the White House and wherever else she stopped on the road trip to Washington, D.C.

Chapter 3

India and Kenya listened attentively as Carmen told them more about London. Everything seemed so cool. Carmen was excited to share all she could about her home. Before you knew it, the girls were planning trips to London in their minds.
"India, we should ask Mom about visiting London," Kenya blurted out.
"I was thinking the same thing, Sis."
"Yes! And when you do, let me know so we can hang out," Carmen replied.
"Hold on! Before I go to London, I have to know, what kinds of food do you have there?" India asked.
"Really India!"
Kenya said, raising her eyebrow at her sister.
Between the two, India was the foodie. She never hesitated to try new foods when they went to different restaurants.

She loved all things breakfast but would try just about anything once. Carmen told them all about fish and chips, pie and mash, full English breakfast, Eton mess, and Yorkshire pudding.

"Shh girls, keep it down," Mom said as she made her way over with the donuts.
"Sorry Mom," the girls replied.
"Mom, this is our new friend, Carmen," said Kenya.
"Yeah, and she came all the way from London."
"It's very nice to meet you Carmen. I'll let you girls continue to talk."

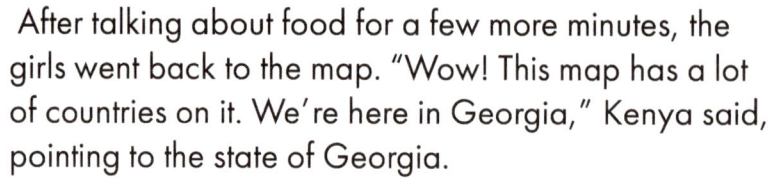

After talking about food for a few more minutes, the girls went back to the map. "Wow! This map has a lot of countries on it. We're here in Georgia," Kenya said, pointing to the state of Georgia.

"Carmen, show us where you live."

"London is right about here," Carmen replied, pointing to her country.

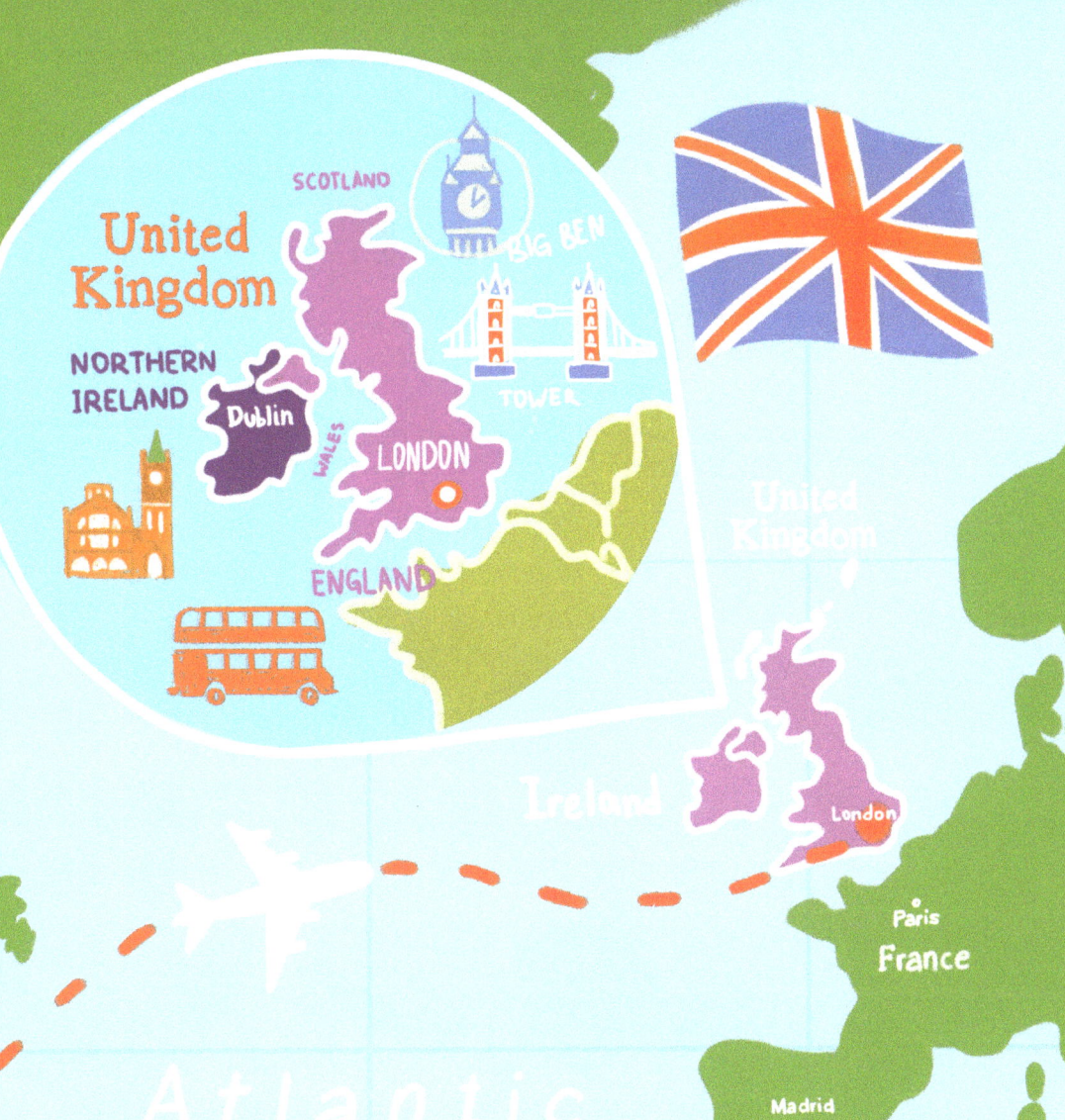

"Wow! That's a long way from here and a long time on an airplane," said India.
"I have been to other places in the States too; like Disney World, New York, and the Grand Canyon. This summer has been amazing," said Carmen.
"We have been to those places, too!" Kenya said.
Then the girls began to talk about the things they saw when they visited the places.

Carmen went on to tell the sisters about all of her travels when she's on holiday. She told them about her trips to Paris, Iceland, and Switzerland.

"Wow! That's cool! It sounds like so much fun traveling to other parts of the world," Kenya replied.

"It really is amazing to see the world, Kenya. I get to hear and learn other languages, explore other cultures, and try different kinds of food."

"Food! What kind of food?" said India with wide eyes.

"Well, the last time I was in Paris, I tried snails in butter for the first time. It was mushy. And I had some yummy buttery croissants with jam."

"Ew! No thanks to slimy, ugly snails, but I would try the buttery croissants! Yum!"

Chapter 4

The girls were so busy talking about food that they didn't notice Carmen's mom walk over to them.
"Hello girls," Carmen's mom said.
"Mum, these are my new friends, India and Kenya."
"Nice to meet you girls. How are the donuts?"
"Good!" the girls responded.
"Alright, well Carmen, I like that you've made new friends, but we have to get back to your grandparent's house before it gets too late."
"Aww," the girls replied in unison. None of them wanted their time together to end. Carmen's mom could see the sadness of having to leave each other in their eyes.

"Don't worry"—she chimed in happily, we'll visit again soon. Girls, where is your mother? I would like to meet her."
"Oh look, she's walking over now," India said, pointing at her mom.
The mothers introduced themselves and exchanged numbers while the girls continued to talk for a few more minutes. Although they overheard their moms setting up a play date, they were still sad when it was officially time to go their separate ways.
"Bye Carmen!" said India and Kenya.
"See you later India and Kenya!" replied Carmen as she waved goodbye.

Chapter 5

The girls couldn't stop thinking about meeting Carmen and talking about the food and all the places she'd visited. Eventually, they wanted to know if their mom had seen other parts of the world. Kenya was the first to speak.

"Mom, have you ever been to London?"
"No girls, I have not been to London, but I have always wanted to go. It is so much fun visiting other countries, trying different foods, and learning about different cultures.

«When I was younger, your grandparents took your aunts and me out of the country once a year. Every year we had to save money and do research on the places we wanted to go the following year.

"It was so exciting to learn about people in other countries."
"Where did you go?" asked Kenya.
"What countries did you visit? India added.
"We went to Spain, Greece, Bali, Cameroon, Japan, and Dubai, just to name a few."

"I can't believe it Mom. Why haven't you taken us to any of these places?" asked India in disbelief.

"Well girls, your father and I wanted to wait until you were old enough to appreciate visiting these countries so you wouldn't only have the memories of it, but could research and learn about them just like your aunts and I did."

"Wow! Well, we're ready!" India said joyfully.

"Yes! I'm definitely going to start researching places when we get home."

"I think London should be the first place we visit since we already have a friend there," Kenya stated.

"Well, that sounds like a plan. Let your dad and me know what you come up with this evening at dinner," Mom replied.

"Yayyyyyyy!" the girls said.

This was going to be one of the most exciting homework assignments ever. The girls couldn't wait to get home.

Chapter 6

Later that evening, Mr. Winter came home from a long day at work.
The girls were in their bedroom researching the London trip so they could present it to their parents at dinner.
"Hello honey, how was your day?" Mr. Winter said after he kissed his wife on her cheek.
"Hey babe, it was really good. I took the girls to that new bookstore, Global Café, and they loved it. They especially loved the donuts."
"I bet! Did you get me anything?"
"I sure did! I got you a butternut donut."
"You know me so well! I love my home state of Tennessee! Thank you! You're the best!"

"You're welcome. Oh, by the way, they met a girl from London at the Global Café. They had so much fun talking to her. The girls told me they talked about various foods and things to do there and started asking me about traveling.
They're upstairs right now researching more about London and will most likely ask to go there."

"Oh, I can't wait to hear what they've learned."
"Me too. I'm so glad they're interested in traveling. It was the highlight of my childhood."
"I agree! I think the girls are old enough now to appreciate it. Let's make a plan and get to it."
"Okay. Dinner will be ready in five minutes. Go ahead and freshen up honey."

Chapter 7

Before the girls knew it, their mom was calling them down for dinner. They'd had enough time to do their research and came up with some great reasons to make London their first visit.

They washed their hands for dinner, went downstairs, and sat at the table.

"Okay girls let's bow our heads for grace," said Dad.

"Dear God, bless this food. May it be nourishment to our bodies, and bless the hands that prepared this wonderful meal. In Jesus' name we pray. Amen!" "Amen!" everyone replied.

"So how was your day, girls?" Mr. Winter asked.
"It was amazing Dad," Kenya replied.
"Mom took us to the Global Café and we met a new friend. Her name is Carmen, and she's from London. She was telling us about all the places she's traveled to in the States, that's what they call the United States—and around the world. Dad, have you traveled outside of the country before?"
"Yes, I have traveled a bit."

"Well, we want to travel too Dad. Mom said you guys were waiting until we were older, but we're older now, and ready," India blurted out.
"Yes! We already know someone who lives there, and it doesn't take that long to get there—only nine hours. If we get our tickets now, round-trip flights only cost $400."
The girls were talking excitedly about all the reasons they should go to London while their parents listened attentively.
"Oh wow! Your mother and I agree that you should. I'm proud of you girls for doing your research. We can save up and plan to go next summer."

"I have some money in my savings account," Kenya said. "Yes! And I have some in my piggy bank too," India replied. "Thanks for offering, but no need for you to touch your savings. Your mom and I have got this. Just continue to keep your grades up and do your chores around the house, and we'll make it happen," Dad said with a wink.

"Yasssssss!" the girls exclaimed. "THIS IS SO AWESOME! THANKS MOM AND DAD!"
"I can't eat anymore," said India excitedly. "I'm ready to plan our trip. May we be excused?"
"Sure girls," Mom replied.
"Aye we're travelers, aye we're travelers," the girls sang as they headed upstairs.

Author Biography

Ericka Mapson was raised in Fort Washington, MD. She is the fourth child and has two brothers and two sisters. Her family of seven traveled domestically visiting many states, but never ventured into international travel. Ericka has always been a creative dreamer. When she graduated from the University of Maryland Eastern Shore with a degree in Hotel and Restaurant Management, a friend from college invited her to visit Germany, and that is when the travel bug hit. She fell in love with traveling to various countries, seeing great sights, experiencing new cultures, and trying adventurous activities. The travel experience has opened her eyes to a whole new world.

Ericka would like to encourage children to travel internationally with their parents or guardians and experience the world with family.

Her favorite motto is,

LIVE IN THE moment

So, get your passport and let's go!

www.ingramcontent.com/pod-product-compliance
Lightning Source LLC
LaVergne TN
LVHW072012060526
838200LV00011B/336